Original title:
A House Built of Dreams

Copyright © 2025 Creative Arts Management OÜ
All rights reserved.

Author: Alec Donovan
ISBN HARDBACK: 978-1-80587-089-0
ISBN PAPERBACK: 978-1-80587-559-8

Cascades of Courage

In a place where socks have fun,
And the forks run marathons,
Brooms dance in the setting sun,
While dust bunnies sing their songs.

Walls whisper secrets of the past,
With squeaky floors that like to tease,
Chasing shadows that run too fast,
While the window giggles in the breeze.

A cat conducts a jazz band here,
While curtains sway like they're on stage,
Mice wear hats and drink their beer,
In this curious, lively cage.

So leap with joy, and don't be shy,
In this wacky maze of delight,
Where dreams take wing and laughter flies,
And every day feels just so right.

Corners of Creativity

In the corner, a cat's pondering,
With dreams of fish and mice wandering.
Four crayons engaged in a dance,
While the walls are making their chance.

A teapot sings the blues with style,
While the rug starts to giggle a while.
A pencil draws a mustache wide,
As the shelves break into a playful slide.

The Ceiling of Serenity

The ceiling fans whirl with great delight,
Chasing dust bunnies into the night.
A light bulb flickers a goofy grin,
While shadows waltz; let the fun begin!

A moonbeam slips through the curtain's fold,
Whispers secrets that never get old.
Laughter echoes in the midnight air,
As the carpet joins the jig with flair.

Spaces Between Thoughts

In the spaces where thoughts collide,
A sofa's laughter cannot hide.
The coffee's brewing quite absurd,
While a to-do list makes a bird.

Between the tweaks of mind and plans,
Pillows burst into silly dance.
A thought takes flight like a kite,
As giggles twinkle in the light.

The Sanctuary of the Soul

In this sanctuary soft and bright,
Socks and shoes hold a wrestling fight.
A clock tick-tocks in funky beats,
As the chair spins, no one retreats.

The walls bubble with stories to share,
While spaghetti noodles float in the air.
A cactus cracks jokes, sharp and tall,
In this refuge where we laugh at all.

Beams from Beyond

In a hut made of hopes and quirky schemes,
The walls dance wildly with electric dreams.
Cats in hard hats, they plan their pursuit,
While mice in bow ties perform a small flute.

A roof of giggles, it sways in delight,
As socks and shoes take off in their flight.
Under the stars, with marshmallows in hand,
We'll roast some laughter, isn't life grand?

The Realm of Resilience

With bricks of humor and mortar of cheer,
This place of whims holds nothing to fear.
A door that squeaks is just saying hello,
And windows wink cheerfully at the show.

Floorboards that creak have stories to share,
Like gossiping squirrels, an odd sort of pair.
In rooms filled with nonsense, joy finds its way,
Building resilience, come join the play!

A Constellation of Comfort

In the galaxy of cuddles and sweet retreat,
Pillows of fluff under wobbly feet.
Stars have faces carved from goodnight tales,
While the fridge hums softly, spinning out gales.

Mismatched socks throw a wild dance party,
Where no one cares who's loud or just farty.
This orbit of joy spins faster each day,
In constellations where silliness stays.

Skylines of Solace

In a skyline of silliness, kites take their flight,
With giggles that soar into the night.
Chimneys that puff out cotton candy dreams,
Waterfalls flowing with chocolate streams.

The rooftops are warm and covered in fluff,
Where clouds chuckle down, saying, "Enough's just enough!"
Sunshine spills in through cracks in the walls,
Creating a canvas where laughter enthralls.

The Cradle of Courage

In the attic, I found a hat,
That claimed to make me a combat brat.
With cape and boots, I charged outside,
To scare the squirrels, I must abide.

But oh, the mailman gave a yell,
Was I the hero? Couldn't tell!
I tripped on grass, fell on my rear,
Yet laughter echoed, washed my fear.

A cardboard sword, my trusty side,
In battles fierce, I would abide.
Each wooden stick, a magic wand,
With giggles loud, I just responded.

So cheers to dreams, inside these walls,
With every laugh, the hero calls.
We dance on floors of makeshift plots,
In my brave world, I fear not monsters' thoughts!

Hearths of Harmony

In the kitchen, pots begin to clank,
As I mix a brew, not top-notch drank.
A dash of sugar, a pinch of spice,
And a whole lot of what's not so nice.

My cookies flopped, a gooey mess,
They looked like art, but caused distress.
The dog enjoyed his tasty prize,
While I just buried my baking lies.

In my living room, we gather near,
With blankets draped, we share our cheer.
A board game night, some "friendly" fights,
Who needs the rules? We'll just take bites!

So here's to harmony, our fun retreat,
With laughter flowing, life is sweet.
In every room, the joy abounds,
With silly antics, harmony surrounds!

Shadows of Serenity

In a corner, shadows play pretend,
Making friends, they never offend.
Ghostly shapes jump on the walls,
With silly dances, each one sprawls.

I wave to them, they giggle back,
In our secret world, we leave no lack.
From broomsticks turned to magic flights,
We soar like stars on silly nights.

A shadow cat curls on my lap,
Dreaming of fish, and perhaps a nap.
With every twitch and playful leap,
Serenity's bonds run oh-so-deep.

So shadows twirl in grace divine,
In this silly realm, all is fine.
With smiles and giggles we share our space,
In the quiet hush, there's joy we embrace!

The Marvel of Make-Believe

In the backyard, a kingdom blooms,
With flowers, weeds, and castle rooms.
A garden hose, a royal stream,
Where all are welcome to live the dream.

A crown of leaves atop my head,
With sticks for wands and none for dread.
I rule the land of universal fun,
Where dragons live, and we all run!

We dance with gnomes and sing with frogs,
While spinning tales of silly logs.
Each rock's a treasure, each tree a friend,
In this wild world, we never end.

So leap with me, let's dare to play,
In our make-believe, we're here to stay.
With laughter bright, our crowns hold tight,
In dreams we find our heart's delight!

Sanctuaries of Spirit

In a fort made of pillows, we reign,
A kingdom of snacks, our sweet domain.
Invisible squirrels throw acorn snacks,
While couch cushions guard against all attacks.

A sock puppet army stands on patrol,
Leading the charge with a potato roll.
Laughter erupts as we plot our next feat,
With giggles and crumbs beneath our retreat.

The ceiling's a sky where daydreams take flight,
While giggling clouds bring us pure delight.
A magical realm where we can explore,
With a wild imagination, who could ask for more?

With crayons and glitter, we craft our grand schemes,
In our sanctuary filled with whimsical dreams.
Let the world outside do its serious thing,
In our snug little haven, we're always king!

Echoes of Endeavor

In the garage, my workshop awaits,
Tools and trinkets, oh, the fascinating fates!
I build flying cars, and they sometimes flop,
But a tumble or two just makes me pop!

I measure with laughter, not with a line,
Each miscalculation makes the journey divine.
Friends gather 'round, bumping elbows and knees,
We take on the world, powered by cheese!

A rocket from soda cans leads to wild air,
A blast of confetti, but did I just swear?
In our lab of inventions, the chaos is grand,
Success tastes sweet, but failure's quite bland.

So let's toast to our dreams, both brilliant and strange,
In the echoes of effort, we'll find room to change.
Here in our playground of goofy delight,
Let's aim for the moon, in our fresh flight!

Dreams Dressed in Dappled Light

A treehouse adorned with glittery flair,
Teacups for seats and a hammock to share.
With a world made of candy and jellybean floors,
We dance through the clouds with umbrella doors.

The sunbeams tickle as we swing high,
While the shadows below have a sneaky spy.
A pinata dragon seeks candy-filled loot,
We giggle and bounce with our bright, funky suit.

Raccoon-tailed cats join our whimsical game,
As we chase down the moon, oh, what a fame!
In a kingdom of laughter where all can unwind,
Our fanciful dreams are never confined.

Each giggle a whisper of sunlight we borrow,
In moments of play, there's no room for sorrow.
With dappled rays painting our glorious scene,
We leap into joy, while the world stays serene!

Lighthouses of Longing

In a fort made of blankets, under the stars,
Pirate ships sailing past Mars!
A map made of dessert with treasure so sweet,
And alligators dance with their tiny feet!

Whispers of wishes carried by light,
As we ride on a comet, oh, what a sight!
Ghosts of the jellybeans guide us tonight,
In lighthouses glowing, we're taking flight.

With laughter our compass, we wander and roam,
In our ports of imaginary home.
A splash of confetti, our victory song,
In this harbor of dreams, we all belong!

So raise up your flag, decked out in cheer,
In this lighthouse of longing, there's nothing to fear.
With friends by our side and adventures anew,
We navigate worlds, so many to view!

The Architecture of Aspirations

In a cottage made of wishes,
Naps are always on the list.
Chocolate fountains, endless gigs,
And mismatched socks that coexist.

Tall towers of pizza stacks,
Here, cheese is the crown of kings.
With pillows for the throne,
We laugh at all the silly things.

Blueprints drawn in crayon hues,
No architect quite like our dreams.
With play-pretend as our muse,
Nothing's ever what it seems.

Join us in our jumbled space,
Where laughter echoes through the walls.
We'll dance on clouds at our pace,
And take the laughs that life installs.

Gardens of the Heart

In our garden, weeds wear hats,
They think they're stylish, oh so grand.
Sunflowers dance with lazy cats,
And bumblebees play in the sand.

Rabbits barter dreams for snacks,
And flowers gossip 'neath the sun.
Each plant enrolls in acting classes,
For the next big show is just for fun.

Garden gnomes hang out for laughs,
Each with their quirks, a funny standoff.
They plot their pranks and silly drafts,
While daisies giggle at the scoff.

Under moonlight, stories bloom,
Of creatures wild, both big and small.
In this plot, there's always room,
For every heart to have a ball.

The Doorway to Desire

Step through a door of marshmallow fluff,
Where wishes slide on buttered toast.
Each twist and turn is sweet and tough,
And giggles linger, coast to coast.

A welcome mat of wanton cheer,
Where socks are mismatched by design.
Knobs that giggle when you steer,
And veils of laughs that brightly shine.

Each room a riddle, every nook,
A treasure trove of silly dreams.
With jokesters hiding by the book,
Stealing smiles with cheeky schemes.

So open wide and come inside,
For what you want is always free.
With joy and jokes as our guide,
We'll dance like leaves on a glee spree.

Staircases to the Sky

Up the stairs of cotton candy,
Each step a giggle, one by one.
The banister is made of dandy,
With shadows bouncing, having fun.

Every landing's a surprise,
With rooms of laughter down the way.
The paintings wink and mesmerize,
While we play hide and seek all day.

At the top, a trampoline cloud,
Where dreams float high like kites above.
We bounce and laugh, so carefree and loud,
This staircase leads to joy and love.

So heed the call of that ascent,
With each step, embrace the wild.
Our skyward dance is heaven-sent,
And in our laughter, we're forever wild.

The Abode of Aspirations

In a place with a creaky floor,
Lies a wish list behind the door.
With walls of candy, windows of pies,
It's a haven for hopeful, giggly sighs.

The roof's made of marshmallows, oh so sweet,
Bouncing on clouds, it's a sugar treat.
The garden grows dreams on licorice vines,
Where laughter sprouts up and sunshine shines.

A cat with a monocle guards the gate,
He purrs out the secrets of silly fate.
Whispers of whimsy float in the air,
As we dance through our dreams without a care.

So let's throw a party with gusto and grace,
In this jolly abode, fill the space.
With balloons full of giggles and cake piled high,
Let's toast to the dreams that never say die!

Tapestry of Tomorrow

In a place where the colors never fade,
Fries rain down like confetti made.
With a twist of fate and a dash of fun,
The tapestry dances in the shining sun.

Tomorrow is woven with threads of cheer,
Where every laugh echoes far and near.
A rollercoaster made of licorice twists,
In this joyous land, no one resists!

The squirrels are wearing tiny hats,
As they juggle cupcakes and acrobat cats.
In a world where the ordinary is bizarre,
We paint ourselves as the silly stars.

So grab a paintbrush, let's splash around,
In a merry mess, let's all be crowned.
For in this tapestry, bright and absurd,
The threads of tomorrow are never blurred!

Steps Toward Serenity

On a staircase made of gummy bears,
Each step taken dissolves all cares.
With laughter echoing from floor to floor,
We march toward joy, always wanting more.

The rails are spun sugar, sweet to touch,
Climbing higher brings such a rush.
With giggles and wiggles we make our way,
To a land where silliness holds sway.

At the top sits a fountain of fizzy soda,
Inviting all to dance and goad us.
Sipping bubbles with friends nearby,
In this quirky haven, we touch the sky.

So let's skip the worries, let them slide,
On these delightful steps, let's take a ride.
For each step we take, through laughter and cheer,
Leads to serenity wrapped in fun and beer!

Windows to Wonder

Peeking through windows of this crazy place,
See waffles flipping in a dreamy space.
They flap their wings and soar so high,
In a land of smiles where we can fly.

Glass panes of jelly wobble with glee,
As we gaze at the wonders, just you and me.
Unicorns frolic on fluffy bread hills,
While the air is sweet with candy spills.

Clouds whisper secrets, tickling the air,
Fortune cookies raining, everywhere!
We'll catch our dreams as they tumble down,
Wearing our giggles like a wacky crown.

So open those windows, let laughter pour,
In a world of wonder, let's explore.
For every moment, a surprise awaits,
In this whimsical place, imagine our fates!

Bridges of Belief

Across the stream of silly thought,
A bridge of giggles, lightly wrought.
With planks of whimsy, painted bright,
We skip and jump into the night.

A troll appears with shoes too large,
He offers us a quirky charge.
"To cross this way, you must recite,
The silliest joke and hold on tight!"

Explosive laughter fills the air,
With every joke, a new despair.
The bridge shakes with our joyful screams,
Who knew belief could make us gleam?

So onward we dance, with glee we soar,
As bridges of belief unlock the door.
With every step, we leave behind,
A trail of laughter, unconfined.

Frameworks of Fantasy

In lands where whimsy takes its flight,
Frameworks shimmer, pure delight.
With beams of laughter, walls of cheer,
Each room holds tales we love to hear.

One wall is made of waffles sweet,
Another dances on tiny feet.
The windows blink with playful eyes,
As clouds float by in silly skies.

Here dreams are crafted like fine art,
With crayons held by a giant heart.
And every corner holds a surprise,
Imagination's feast, oh what a prize!

So come and play, don't be so formal,
Let's turn the world into a portal.
In these frameworks, let's take a chance,
To twirl and leap in our own dance.

The Cellar of Secrets

Down in the dark, where whispers creep,
Lies a cellar filled with secrets deep.
Jars of giggles stacked so high,
With silly songs that make you fly.

A bottle spills its funny tales,
Of chickens clucking dressed in veils.
Another swirls with fizzy dreams,
That burst like popcorn, or so it seems.

Each corner holds a quirky find,
A sock that sings, a cat that's blind.
We laugh and shiver in delight,
At secrets shared in the chilly night.

So pop the cork, let laughter ring,
In the cellar, we are kings.
With every joke, a treasure's found,
In shadows where our giggles sound.

The Fount of Fulfillment

Beneath the moon, a fount does bubble,
With bubbly water, all things double.
If you lean in and take a sip,
You might just find your silly trip.

It grants the dreams of joy and fun,
With every drop, a race begun.
A splash of laughter fills the air,
As frogs in hats leap here and there.

Each giggle turns the water gold,
Tales of mishaps yet untold.
And dancing cups dance with delight,
In the fount where dreams take flight.

So raise a glass to silliness bold,
In the fount where we break the mold.
With every laugh, we're whisked away,
To magical lands where we can play.

Shimmering Foundations

In a yard made of marshmallows, I tread,
With candy canes holding up my bed.
Dreams of piñata roofs so bright,
I'll sleep with the giggles deep into the night.

Each wall is a wobbly Jenga stack,
My neighbors all stop by for a snack.
Chandeliers made of glow-in-the-dark toys,
Echoing laughter with all of my joys.

Sofa of squishies, I'll sink right in,
A fridge full of ice cream, let the feast begin!
Carpet of jellybeans, all sticky and wild,
Every room's playground for the young at heart child.

So here's to the wishes that dance in my head,
In a kaleidoscope world, where silliness spreads.
With mirth as my blueprint, I'll dance through each door,
In my whimsical kingdom where joy is the floor.

The Essence of Elysium

In a kitchen where broccoli sings and hops,
The blender mixes up candy pops.
Pancakes flip themselves with flair,
While syrup rains down, without a care.

Walls painted in colors unusual and bright,
Where unicorns party from morning till night.
Light bulbs that giggle when you turn them on,
And chairs that dance to the sound of a yawn.

A bathtub filled with fluffy clouds,
Neighbors try out their happy-like shrouds.
Shower heads shower sprinkles, oh what a treat,
With rubber duck bands making beats so sweet.

So here's to our realm, so silly and free,
Where everyone laughs just like a glee bee.
In every odd corner, let laughter resume,
Creating a wondrous space of cartoonish bloom.

Shadows of Splendor

Cactus-shaped lamps light the funky hall,
With shadows that party and giggle and sprawl.
Dust bunnies dance with a twist and a shout,
In this lively abode of whimsy throughout.

A fridge with a gnome who tells silly jokes,
Where milk cartons wear hats like rogue little folks.
Floorboards that creak with a musical hint,
Play tunes that inspire spontaneous sprint.

Each window a canvas where silliness thrives,
With birds playing chess and beehives in dives.
A toaster that pops out toast in the air,
While waffles take selfies, with not a care.

So here's to the shadows, with laughter so grand,
In every odd nook, we twirl and we stand.
Life is a jest, in this land of the fun,
Where the sun beam winks, till the day is done.

The Architecture of Ambitions

My blueprint's a riddle with no end in sight,
Where kites fly to rooftops from morning till night.
A door made of giggles swings wide open,
Welcoming dreams that may seem unspoken.

Slide down the staircase, it's really a slide,
Rocket ships parked where the brooms reside.
In this madcap realm where we dare to believe,
Whimsical wonders are ours to weave.

My ceiling's a trampoline, bouncing out dreams,
With glittering stars and eccentric schemes.
Living in laughter, we plot and we plan,
For each curl of a smile sparks joy in the span.

So here's to the dreams that tickle our toes,
In this slightly absurd, most fun saga flows.
Building ambitions with joy and delight,
In a carnival world, everything feels right.

Foundations of Fantasy

In a yard where giggles grow,
We stack our dreams, just so you know.
With marshmallow bricks and jelly bean glue,
Our castle's ready for a party, too!

Giant socks make up the walls,
And pickle jars are our sound calls.
A trampoline roof for bouncing delight,
Who needs sleep? We'll dream all night!

Raccoon guards at the front door,
With a welcome sign that asks for more.
Claiming our space in a colorful mess,
In this silly fortress, we feel blessed!

Swinging from chandeliers made of string,
Our laughter echoes, oh what a swing!
In this realm of nonsensical schemes,
Here's to a life built on whimsical dreams!

Walls of Whispers

The walls around us hum and chatter,
With tales of giggles and friendly banter.
They hide our secrets beneath a disguise,
With fairy lights twinkling in their eyes.

Pillow fights break through the silence,
While ferrets dance in a wild alliance.
The paint peels off with a playful twist,
A masterpiece made of things we missed.

Post-its flutter like butterflies,
Carrying wishes that soar to the skies.
Chasing shadows that paint the floor,
Our walls have stories we've yet to explore!

When night falls, the walls become lively,
As we chase our dreams with a dash of jive!
Each creak and each crack reveals a new tune,
In a cozy symphony beneath the moon.

Windows to Tomorrow

With windows wide to see what's next,
We peer through frames, feeling perplexed.
A boiling cauldron of dreams on the stove,
Brewing ideas like a mischievous cove.

The curtains are clouds, fluffy and bright,
Trailing rainbows through the night.
With a wink from the stars, they give us a shove,
To leap forward with dreams we love!

Framed in laughter, our sights are set,
Planning to catch our dreams in a net.
Each glance reveals what could be done,
Painting the world with the light of the sun.

So let's climb through each pane of delight,
And explore the wonders hidden from sight.
Tomorrow shines through with vibrant beams,
In our playful jaunt of endless dreams!

The Blueprint of Hope

Map out our laughter, sketch a delight,
Where dreams take shape, ready for flight.
With crayons and giggles in hand we mix,
Twirling through plans like a wild dancing fix.

Each room a canvas, each corner a joke,
A space where dreams and laughter evoke.
Draw more cupcakes than you could eat,
While rainbows invest in our fun little feat.

Blueprints of hope drawn in jelly stain,
With unicorns leaping through a candy cane lane.
We fold our wishes and set them afloat,
On a paper boat that laughs as it wrote.

So here's to the plans, funny and bright,
In our whimsical world, we'll take flight.
With laughter as ink and dreams as our guide,
We'll build our magical life, full of pride!

Roofs of Reverie

Cushions float like clouds in air,
With popcorn roofs and jelly chair.
The windows blink, they wink and sway,
While squirrels dance at noon each day.

Dreams slide down a rainbow slide,
With candy walls too thick to hide.
The frogs croak tunes of jazz and cheer,
As disco lights make curtains clear.

A cat in boots takes center stage,
Reciting lines from an old page.
The fish swim tales of far-off lands,
While unicorns play in the sands.

With pillows soft and laughter loud,
Each guest a quirky, fun-filled crowd.
In this abode of giggles free,
Life dances wildly—come and see!

The Sanctuary of Stardust

In a room where laughter reigns,
Socks wear hats and dance in trains.
The walls are lined with silly hats,
And cats in boots play chess with rats.

A trampoline of dreams so high,
Gives bouncing shoes a chance to fly.
The jellies jiggle, strut their stuff,
While magic wands declare, "Enough!"

The ceiling drips with lemon pie,
And cupcakes spin through paths up high.
Here, wishes bubble like a stew,
With rainbows sprouting right on cue.

Where ice cream showers last till dawn,
And giggles echo like a song.
This land of whimsy, fun, and cheer,
Is where the heart holds all that's dear.

Pillars of Possibility

Pillars made of candy cane,
Stand tall against a world of rain.
Chocolate rivers flow with glee,
While marshmallow clouds make tea for three.

Here, penguins wear a dapper tie,
And ride tricycles beneath the sky.
Lions paint their manes and roar,
As laughter spills right through the door.

Each doorway's framed with jokes and cheer,
Accentuating every year.
With doors that swing both ways, it's true,
Anyone can join the crew!

Here, wishes grow like flowers wild,
As each played tune brings out the child.
In this realm of giggles bright,
Adventure beckons, pure delight!

Halls of Heartfelt Hopes

In halls where joy is on display,
A painting laughs, a potpourri play.
Bananas wear their finest shoes,
And jelly beans dodge daily snooze.

Here, every wall whispers delight,
Making shadow puppets dance at night.
The ceiling hums a silly tune,
As paper planes all swoop in June.

Dreams leap high off trampoline beds,
Where pillow fights replace our dreads.
The laughter flows like sweetened tea,
In this wild labyrinth of glee.

On every shelf, a treasure rests,
Stories, lip-syncs, silly tests.
With hearts wide open, dreams take flight,
In these amusing halls of light!

Enchanted Entrance

Step right up, don't be shy,
Where socks can dance, and cats can fly.
The doorbell sings a silly tune,
While gnomes do yoga 'neath the moon.

With hats all crooked, and shoes askew,
The hallway giggles, welcoming you.
A carpet that tickles your toes,
And walls that tell secrets nobody knows.

In the kitchen, a pot's lost its lid,
While spoons are playing hide and seek, they did.
Cookies bounce in a laughter spree,
And toast pops up, yelling, "Pick me!"

So here's the key to this mad abode,
Where floppy hat dreams are freely bestowed.
Join the fun in this whimsical place,
With chuckles and quirks, it's a laugh-filled space.

The Windowsill of Wisdom

Upon the sill, a wise old snail,
Spins yarns of cheese and a fluffy tail.
He preaches patience, while munching on greens,
In a world of nonsense, he reigns as the queen.

A frog with glasses recites a rhyme,
While number 7 learns to climb.
They debate life's woes with a cup of tea,
And chuckle at how odd it can be.

A spider weaves jokes into its threads,
Tickling the ears of sleepy heads.
They giggle and squirm, not a care in sight,
As the sun waves goodnight, taking flight.

The window's a portal, both strange and sweet,
Where dreams hatch cookies to rise on their feet.
Join the party of critters, don't delay,
For wisdom comes best when it's shared in play.

Laughter in the Lattice

Tangled vines with a flair for fun,
Whispering jokes beneath the sun.
They tickle the fence and wiggle about,
Making even the grumpiest pout.

A squirrel dressed up in a tiny hat,
Recites a poem to a curious cat.
They chuckle together, rolling in delight,
As butterflies join in, flapping so bright.

The lattice is buzzing, it's quite the sight,
Where shadows dance and lanterns light.
A chorus of giggles wafts through the air,
As flowers gossip without a care.

So lift your spirits and join the cheer,
In this patch of laughter, hold dear.
For in the lattice where silliness reigns,
Life's quirks are celebrated, devoid of chains.

Dreams on the Threshold

At the doorstep lies a dream so bold,
Made of jelly beans and tales of old.
With a welcome mat that wiggles and grins,
It opens up doors to absurd wins.

A pair of slippers that dance with flair,
Invite you in for a whimsical dare.
With each step forward, a giggle escapes,
As the ceiling drips chocolate and shapes.

In the corner, a chair croons offbeat tunes,
While under the rug, a llama festoons.
It's a frolicsome gathering of the odd,
Where weirdness is cherished, and laughter's a nod.

So tiptoe inside, let go of your frowns,
And join the parade of peculiar clowns.
For dreams on the threshold are meant to be shared,
In this land of the silly, you'll never be scared.

The Gables of Growth

In the attic, a pot of gold,
With marshmallows, I'll be bold.
The squirrels keep stealing my pie,
But they dance like they can fly.

Windows wide, where laughter spills,
And giggles echo from the hills.
A garden gnome with a funny hat,
Claims he's got a petting cat.

Walls with stories, painted bright,
Crying onions under moonlight.
The floorboards squeak a laugh or two,
As if they have a joke for you.

With each room, a different scheme,
In my world of silly dreams.
I'll host a party on the roof,
For chattering birds, that's the proof.

Footsteps of Faith

Each step echoes with a grin,
As I trip over my own chin.
With socks that clash like bright sun rays,
I dance my way through silly days.

The hallway's lined with love and cheer,
And every corner holds a beer.
I'll leap and twirl, embrace the chance,
In my mismatched socks, I prance.

Each door creaks softly, whispers low,
About the times I've been a show.
My cat thinks she's the queen of all,
She's plotting from her royal hall.

The staircase leads to pies in air,
And laughter floats without a care.
In this place of whimsy's race,
I conquer life with joyous grace.

The Oasis of Openness

A living room as bright as cheer,
Where every couch can spin and steer.
A blender sings, a toast it makes,
To all the crazy, fun mistakes.

The fridge is stocked with dreams so sweet,
With chocolate mountains, oh what a treat!
My friends all gather, silly hats,
We share hot cocoa, and friendly chats.

A window offers views of jest,
As squirrels perform their wild best.
I cheer them on, with popcorn flung,
At their daring leaps, I'm always sprung.

In this space of cozy glee,
I find my joy is just to be.
With laughter echoing from the floor,
Each moment's magic—who could ask for more?

The Sunlit Sanctuary

Sunbeams waltz on every wall,
With socks that sparkle at the ball.
I juggle dreams like oranges bright,
And laugh at shadows in the light.

A rooftop where my imagination flies,
I sail on clouds that wave goodbyes.
My imaginary friends debate,
Who's the best at juggling fate.

The floors adorned with wacky glue,
Paint splatters that tell tales anew.
Each canvas whispers, paints in jest,
Of all our silly, wild quests.

In this haven where giggles bloom,
I dance with sunlight, embrace the room.
For every corner plans a joke,
In this sanctuary, dreams invoke.

Pillows of Peace

On a mountain of cushions, I lay down my head,
Feathers of laughter dance, dreams lightly spread.
With a blanket of giggles, I drift off to play,
In my castle of whimsy, come join me, they say.

The walls are all painted with shades of delight,
Where shadows of silliness frolic at night.
A ceiling of joy that hums soft lullabies,
As I snooze on a cloud, with snickers, I rise.

Cats play confetti, and dogs pass the snacks,
A party of plush toys, no reason to relax.
The fridge is a treasure of candies galore,
In this funny little realm, who could ask for more?

With slippers that giggle and curtains that sway,
I'll bounce on this mattress and laugh the day away.
So come one, come all, let's all take a leap,
In my kingdom of dreams, we'll never lose sleep.

Retrospectives of Radiance

Under a disco ball, my memories swirl,
With colors of joy that twirl and unfurl.
Old jokes echo softly, like whispers in tune,
A time capsule dancing beneath a bright moon.

The walls of my brain are graffiti of cheer,
With sketches of high-fives and laughter sincere.
Every corner reveals a smile caught in frame,
Where the fun times of yesteryears still claim their fame.

Nostalgic adventures on slides made of dreams,
Where laughter erupts in whimsical themes.
With bouncing bear hugs and musical springs,
My past is a carnival, where joy always sings.

So let's raise a toast to the fun that we've had,
To the silly, the weird, to the wonderfully mad.
In this retrospective, we splurge and we play,
With a wink to tomorrow in our fanciful way.

Nestled in Nostalgia

In a nook of my heart, where the funny things stay,
Tickles and giggles just won't go away.
A treasure chest filled with capers of old,
Where every sardonic glance has a story retold.

Grandpa's old stories of mischief and gaffes,
Mixing legends of giants with unintended laughs.
A slip on a banana, the slide of a shoe,
Memories like fireworks light up the preview.

The attic holds secrets, a saxophone cat,
Singing off-key while sitting on a mat.
With shelves stacked with moments, we laugh at the flaws,
As joy waddles by, waving its paws.

So let's cozy up in this nostalgia spree,
With dreams interwoven like threads of glee.
In this whimsical corner, we'll never grow old,
For laughter and friendship are treasures untold.

The Illumination of Imaginations

There's a spark in my mind, a little bright light,
Where doodles become tales that dance in the night.
Imagination bounces, as bright as can be,
Painting rainbows on walls of possibility.

In a world made of marshmallows, where teapots can sing,

I'm the monarch of whimsy, with a crown made of spring.

The trees hold surprises, like hats in the breeze,
With squirrels in tuxedos requesting some cheese.

Mirrors reflect laughter through windows of glee,
As I ride on a pelican soaring the sea.
With jellybean paths that twinkle and hum,
Every thought is a party—come join the fun!

So let's soar on the wings of whatever we choose,
In this illuminated land, we'll never lose.
For the magic of dreaming is ours to embrace,
In a universe spun from a joyful, kind place.

Shadows of Solace

In the attic, a ghost with a grin,
Sips lemonade while the chaos spins.
With mismatched chairs and floors so creaky,
Every corner holds tales that are cheeky.

The walls whisper jokes when the moon's out bright,
A chandelier swings, just dodging a bite.
Dust bunnies dance like they're on the run,
In this quirky nook, we find our fun.

When shadows get silly, they tumble and play,
They twist and they turn, making night into day.
With laughter echoing, fears start to flee,
Oh, what a place, this odd little spree.

Every crack holds a memory or two,
Of socks on the ceiling and odd things we do.
In shadows of solace, our laughter takes flight,
In a home full of dreams, everything feels right.

The Framework of Wishes

Nails and boards are wishing on stars,
Crafted hopes wrapped in candy bars.
A framework built with giggles and glue,
Making magic with mischief anew.

Stairs that squeak like a ticklish mouse,
Doorbells that giggle when folks come to browse.
Floors made of marshmallows, soft and so sweet,
In this wishful world, everyone we meet.

Windows that wink when the sun starts to rise,
Curtains that play hide and seek with our eyes.
In every corner, a silly surprise,
The framework's alive with laughter and sighs.

With each funny twist, every turn seems so grand,
A place where dreams grow just like a band.
In a home filled with wishes, joy knows no end,
Where silliness reigns and hearts can transcend.

Hearth of Humanity

In the kitchen, a bubbling pot sings,
Of dancing spoons and joy that it brings.
A hearth where burnt toast turns into delight,
And laughter erupts like fireworks at night.

Cookies with faces, all frosted with cheer,
Whispering secrets that only we hear.
The cat in the hat juggles fish from a bowl,
In this human hearth, we nourish the soul.

With quilts made of stories and warmth in our hearts,
Every meal shared is where love truly starts.
In the warmth of the hearth, we gather and play,
Creating a magic that brightens the day.

Through silly mistakes, we all come together,
In aprons of joy, we withstand any weather.
In the hearth of humanity, we find our flair,
Where laughter is plenty and joy fills the air.

Hallways of Happiness

In hallways of happiness, tickles abound,
Footsteps are giggling without making a sound.
Posters of puns hang on every bare wall,
A maze of good vibes that invites us to drawl.

Every turn brings a joke or a tease,
With doors that swing wide, if you just say please.
A rug that rolls up to express its delight,
In these funny hallways, everything feels right.

With echoes of laughter that bounce off the floor,
Each corner a portal to something we adore.
From silly faces caught in a frame,
To whispers of stories that never feel tame.

As we wander through spaces both lively and bright,
In hallways of happiness, all worries take flight.
With smiles in abundance, all worries grow small,
In this cheerful abode, we are happy for all.

The Willows of Wisdom

Under branches, secrets grow,
Squirrels plotting on the low.
Whispers float on breezy tones,
While frogs wear crowns upon their thrones.

The sun shines down, a golden glow,
As crickets sing in splendid row.
Wise old owls keep watchful eyes,
On all the shenanigans of the skies.

Every leaf, a story spun,
In this giggling realm of fun.
Children dance on grass so green,
While dreaming wild—what a scene!

So let's all skip and sing along,
In the willows where we belong.
With laughter echoing through the air,
Here's to wishes without a care!

Atelier of Aspirations

In my studio of bright ideas,
Paint spills like a thousand leers.
Canvas waits with arms so wide,
As I throw colors on the ride.

Brush in hand, I swirl and twirl,
Creating chaos, oh what a whirl!
A ghost haunts as I draft my plans,
While glitter flies like tiny fans.

Friends drop by for a laughing spree,
Painting rainbows, oh so free.
We mix up dreams in pots so round,
The mess we make is profound!

Through splashed paint, we find our goals,
Crafting visions that touch our souls.
This atelier of big dreams loud,
Is where we dance, and we're so proud!

The Theatre of the Dreamt

In the theater of wildest schemes,
Playwrights scribble silly themes.
Actors wear the wackiest hats,
Dancing like confused acrobats.

The curtains rise on a bright green stage,
As cats perform in a fit of rage.
With applause from mice and cheer from birds,
Each scene unfolds without any words.

The plot thickens with a pie fight,
Or a talking tree that's quite the sight.
Audience roars with laughter and glee,
As the stars prance, wild and free.

Final bows with silly face,
In this theater, joy finds its place.
With dreams exchanged through comedic plays,
We leave with smiles that last for days!

The Realm of Reflection

In a land where mirrors laugh aloud,
Reflections dance in a shimmering crowd.
Water glimmers, secrets unfold,
As shadows play with stories bold.

Every glance brings forth a grin,
As mismatched thoughts race and spin.
Frogs wear glasses, inspecting their fate,
While turtles debate over who's late.

Spoilers lurk in puddles so deep,
As puddled dreams take a cheeky leap.
We jump through ripples, twists and turns,
In this realm, the water churns.

So come along, with giggles in sight,
Let's dance with reflections in pure delight.
With every splash, let laughter ring,
In this quirky world where dreams take wing!

Stories Under the Stars

Under a moon that wears a hat,
We chat with a furry, dancing cat.
He spills the tea, then drops his guard,
Claiming he's actually Bard the Bard.

Shooting stars take a coffee break,
While we gaze and make our great mistakes.
Each twinkle winks with a goofy grin,
Whispers secrets where the fun begins.

Laughter bounces across the night,
As giggles echo in soft moonlight.
A jellybean comet zooms past fast,
Leaving us wishing for a magical cast.

In dreams we chase the silly fate,
Then snooze away 'til it's far too late.
Under this sky, forever we'll play,
No need for sleep, let the stars have their say.

Mosaics of Magic

In the corner sits a unicorn lamp,
With a smile bright enough to make a stamp.
Glitter dust on walls does twirl,
As a gnome plays hopscotch with a whirl.

Jellybeans litter the floor with flair,
While kittens in hats dance without a care.
Each color chatters in splendid noise,
Building a world with the hopes of toys.

Rainbows slide down the stairway of dreams,
Echoing laughter as sunlight beams.
Pillows in castles, woven with jokes,
Soak in the whimsy made by the folks.

We paint the day in hues of delight,
With every stroke, we lighten the night.
Here magic lives in the laugh we sing,
Creating mischief from the heart of spring.

Vaulted Vistas of Vision

High above, the ceiling sparkles bright,
With chandeliers made of jelly and light.
We climb on clouds that are fluffy and free,
Building castles out of sheer jubilee.

Silly snails run a race on the wall,
While squirrel acrobats tumble and fall.
Cobbled paths of chocolate trace our steps,
As we learn to dance with the thump and pep.

Galaxies swirl in our cozy nook,
Pages turn themselves from our handmade book.
Every story twists with a giggle and spin,
As the moon winks, ready for mischief to begin.

With visions grand, we paint our dreams bold,
Twirling and laughing, never feeling old.
Each room is a stage in this vault of charm,
Feathers and laughter keep us safe from harm.

The Nest of New Beginnings

In a birdhouse made of cookie dough,
Chirps a wise owl with a dash of a show.
Feathers shake with the tales of the past,
As we splash paint and make memories last.

Nestled in pillows, we throw a roast,
To celebrate dreams and provinces coast.
Ever so gently, the laughter flows,
Mixing with giggles like tickling toes.

With each crack of dawn, we plant a seed,
Of thoughts so bright they're bound to succeed.
A pancake now flies and makes a round trip,
While syrupy myriads do funny flips.

New beginnings dance in jesting delight,
As night falls softly with a wink of light.
We'll toast marshmallows on whimsical beams,
In a nest built sweet with all our dreams.

Roofs of Reverie

The shingles shimmer in my mind,
Where unicorns play and dreams unwind.
A chimney that puffs out candy fluff,
And walls that giggle when times get tough.

The garden grows jellybeans so sweet,
Flowers tap-dance on their happy feet.
Squirrels wear hats and throw a ball,
In this funny world, I'm having a ball!

Windows that wink at the setting sun,
Mirrors that flash and say, 'You're number one!'
The floorboards sing songs of silly cheer,
In this comical haven, it's all crystal clear!

So come on in, take a little chance,
Join in the laughter, come join the dance.
In this funny abode where dreams collide,
You'll find a spot where joy can't hide.

Echoes of Imagination

In the hallway, echoes of a cat,
Chasing shadows, pouncing like that!
The wallpaper whispers jokes at night,
While dancing beds put up a fight.

The staircase speaks in silly rhymes,
A slide instead of steps, oh, how sublime!
Posters of llamas, dressed for a ball,
In this playful space, we'll have a ball!

A bathtub that bubbles with fizzy glee,
Rubber ducks quack in perfect harmony.
The fridge is stocked with ice cream galore,
In this world, who could ask for more?

Cushions that bounce, a floor made of cheese,
Each room invites you to conquer with ease.
With laughter and whimsy, come take a look,
In this echoing realm, you're off the hook!

Pillars of Possibility

Pillars painted in polka dots bright,
Holding up dreams like balloons in flight.
The ceiling's a canvas, a sight to behold,
With stars that giggle and tales to be told.

In the kitchen, the spoons do a jig,
As pots and pans join in the gig.
The fridge opens wide, what a delight,
With snacks that sparkle in the moonlight!

A couch that whispers, 'Come sit for a while',
As the lamp shares secrets with a quirky smile.
The carpet sings songs of funky delight,
In this wacky wonder, everything feels right.

With each corner filled with surprises galore,
Open the door to laughter, explore!
Where anything goes, and you're never alone,
In this whimsical place, you've found your home!

Rooms of Radiance

Rooms filled with light and tickles of air,
Where socks have parties without a care.
The bed has dreams of sugar and spice,
Inviting the giggles, rolling the dice.

In the attic, there's a treasure of hats,
Pirates and wizards, all silly chitchats.
A window that opens to giggling skies,
Where cupcakes rain down and laughter flies.

The bathroom's a spa for rubber duck crew,
With bubbles that burst into a giggly view.
Shampoo serenades while towels hold tight,
In this cheery abode, everything's bright.

Join the fun in this radiant zone,
Where each room sparkles and laughter is sown.
In this lively paradise, come take a glance,
You're sure to be swept away in the dance!

Dreams Adrift in the Attic

In the attic, dust bunnies play,
With big hats on, they dance all day.
Socks with holes have formed a band,
Singing tunes that are quite unplanned.

Old toys giggle when no one's near,
Puppets telling tales of cheer.
A rocking horse dreams of a race,
But trips on a rubber duck's face.

A clock that ticks in reverse time,
Laughs at the chaos, oh so sublime.
Marbles roll with a squeaky sound,
In this attic, joy is found.

So next time you feel kind of blue,
Check the attic, it might help you!
For dreams there drift, light as a feather,
In a haven where laughter gathers.

A Canvas of Comfort

In a room where shadows play,
Painted walls shout 'Hip Hip Hooray!'
Every color has a say,
Even the yellow feels quite gay.

A couch that squeaks when you sit down,
Complains like a child in a frown.
Pillows throwing a feathery fight,
It's a family's humorous delight.

The fridge hums a mischievous tune,
Dreaming of midnight snacks with the moon.
While curtains swing in a playful dance,
Catching sunlight as they prance.

Laughter echoes, bright and loud,
In this warmth, we are all proud.
A canvas built with quirks and charms,
Where smiles wrap us in their arms.

Whispers of Wishes

In the corners whispers roam,
Tick-tock, the clock makes it home.
A wishbone hangs on a cheerful wall,
Waiting for the next big brawl!

Chairs gossip in creaks and squeaks,
Sharing stories of funny peaks.
Each window winks a friendly eye,
While curtains sway and sigh goodbye.

The mirror reflects a cheeky grin,
As if it's laughing at a sin.
While bread in the toaster makes some noise,
Thinking of all its early joys.

So let your wishes softly sip,
On the laughter that life can whip.
For in this space where whispers weave,
Funny tales we all believe.

Foundations of Fantasy

Beneath the floorboards, secrets lie,
A squirrel thinks it's a castle high.
With nuts as treasures, he stands quite bold,
In this realm, he's struck gold!

Walls converse with a sighing sound,
Hoping to hold each joy that's found.
The ceiling dreams of heights untold,
Wishing for clouds and sunshine gold.

Ovens chuckle with a baking spree,
Cookies plotting a wild jubilee.
While the cupboard sings of snacks galore,
Inviting all for a joyful score.

With every corner, laughter beams,
In our fairy tale of vibrant schemes.
For at its base, with a twist of jam,
Lie funny fables, oh how they slam!

The Overture of Optimism

In the attic, hopes are flying,
Got a rubber duck, it's not complying.
The walls are wobbly, the roof's a tease,
Yet in my heart, there's a dancing breeze.

The floorboards creak, they sing a tune,
A diabolical plot with a spoon.
Juggling dreams like they're made of cheese,
Who needs a ladder when you have wheeze?

The windows wink with a glimmer bright,
Shining stars sneak in at night.
Curtains of yarn, a colorful sight,
Pet goldfish claim they can take flight.

With each wobbly step, I giggle, fall,
Creating a mansion from dreams so small.
A place for laughter, and joy to sprawl,
The overture plays, hear the echoing call.

Twilight of Tranquility

In the garden, gnomes hold a show,
Chasing sunbeams like they're on the go.
Butterflies gossip, bees join in too,
While daisies dance, showing off their dew.

The fence is painted in polka-dot bliss,
Socks on the line, a bubbly kiss.
Chairs are wobbly but filled with cheer,
Whispers of calm we can all hear.

A cat with a crown sits on a throne,
Declaring the day as 'cuddle zone.'
Twilight whispers secrets in the breeze,
Tickling the leaves with playful tease.

With fireworks made of old socks and dreams,
We're sailing through moonlit, silvery beams.
Tranquility wraps us in silly lights,
As laughter echoes through magical nights.

The Cultivation of Calm

On a sunny patch, I plant my thoughts,
Wearing flip-flops and mismatched socks.
Sprouting giggles, watered with ice cream,
Dandelions dancing in a puff of dream.

The daisies debate who's the fairest flower,
While butterflies vote every half an hour.
A cabbage pondered the meaning of life,
In the garden where silliness is rife.

I dug with a spoon, brought in a chair,
Invited ants for a party affair.
Together we harvest laughter and song,
In the cultivation of calm, we all belong.

Through tickly grass and bright sunny hues,
We munch on giggles, share silly news.
The fairy lights flicker, the evening's still,
With whispers of joy riding down the hill.

The Palette of Possibilities

With crayons in hand and laughter loud,
I sketch a castle that's proud and unbowed.
A rainbow slide, where unicorns race,
Pillow clouds with a cuddly embrace.

The paintbrush swims in a sea of delight,
Splashing colors like stars in the night.
Cheese wheels spin under a disco ball,
Sardines in tuxedos hold a masquerade ball.

Each stroke is a giggle, a tickling spree,
Painting the world so whimsically free.
A canvas of dreams, that opens our eyes,
In the palette of possibilities, all joy lies.

With every color, a new tale unfurls,
A swirling tornado of giggles and whirls.
In these imaginative lands, come play along,
For life is a canvas; let's make it strong!

The Home of Hope

In a place where wishes wait,
Cats dance on the kitchen plate.
Where coffee brews with midnight's cheer,
And socks play hide-and-seek, my dear.

The fridge holds secrets we can share,
While dust bunnies hold a fair.
Chairs that squeak a comic tune,
And laughing walls that hug the moon.

Here dreams are baked in a pie pan,
With melted cheese, oh what a plan!
The couch holds stories, soft and grand,
With popcorn memories close at hand.

So if you stop by for a while,
Bring your brightest, cheesiest smile.
In this quirky nook, you might find,
A treasure trove of laughter, kind.

Walls Woven from Wisdom

The walls are thick with tales untold,
As creaky floors start to unfold.
A laugh turns into echoing rhyme,
In this whimsical space, it's always prime.

A clock that ticks in fits and starts,
Counts down to laughter, not to parts.
Where wisdom whispers from the shelves,
And all the cups have cozy selves.

With a roof that twirls on sunny days,
And windows that dance in breezy plays.
Each corner holds a joke or pun,
In this tapestry, we all are one.

So come join the fun, and sit awhile,
With stories bold and voices wild.
In this kooky realm, we thrive with ease,
And weave our life with giggles and cheese.

Echoes of Enchantment

In realms where giggles take the lead,
And candy rain delivers speed.
Where tea stains smile on the carpet's face,
And time can't keep up in this goofy space.

The echoes bounce off walls with glee,
As socks reenact a comic spree.
Unicorns prance on the dining chair,
While marshmallow clouds float in the air.

Every nook has a cheeky grin,
With splashes of joy that never thin.
Windsor chairs use wizard's wands,
To move around and cast their fawns.

So visit this realm where dreams collide,
And find the magic we all can ride.
In echoes bright, we'll laugh and cheer,
In this merry haunt, there's naught to fear.

Blueprints of Bliss

On paper blue, we sketch our fun,
With crayons bright, the plans begun.
Each room a giggle, each hall a cheer,
In a layout that brings us all near.

The kitchen hums a tune of pies,
While jars of cookies plot their lies.
Counters that sashay with spice and zest,
Kitchen aids know how to jest.

The attic lives in a pile of dreams,
With stuffed bears talking in moonbeams.
Blueprints scattered with a trail of zest,
Where laughter echoes, we find our rest.

So sketch your joy, let creativity flow,
In this playful place, our hearts aglow.
With whimsical floors and ceilings high,
Join the fun, watch our spirits fly!

Canvas of Contemplation

We paint with colors, oh so bright,
While squirrels debate, in sheer delight.
A roof of thoughts, our musings flow,
As cats in hats prance to and fro.

With dreams like bubbles, we chase them fast,
While shadows laugh, and moments last.
Each brushstroke tickles, igniting cheer,
In our silly realm, nothing to fear.

A missed call echoing, a laugh in vain,
As dreams get tangled, like yarn on a chain.
Pickle jars filled with wishes and glee,
Who knew our imaginations were so free?

Laughter hangs like a canvas wide,
Where ridiculous visions cheerfully reside.
Let's tiptoe through whims, so grand and bright,
In this merry maze, everything's just right.

The Sphere of Serenity

In a world of giggles and floating hats,
Bumblebees gossip, and no one chats.
Kites dance with laughter in a silent breeze,
While unicorns sip tea beneath the trees.

Chasing jellybeans on a cloudy day,
As tumbleweeds dance in a whimsical way.
We build our realm with jelly and cream,
In this round place, life's a funny dream.

Turtles racing in a slow-motion fight,
With daydreams bursting, oh what a sight!
The floorboards creak with a merriment tune,
As we twirl and spin beneath a green moon.

The sphere rolls on, with giggles and grace,
Where every mishap adds charm to the space.
With feathers of laughter and magic galore,
This sphere of tranquility opens a door.

The Echo Chamber of Envisioned Lives

Echoes of laughter, bouncing around,
As thoughts collide, in joy they abound.
We juggle our dreams, with banana flair,
While socks on our heads float high in the air.

Pancakes whisper secrets, syrupy and sweet,
In this chamber of quirks, nothing's discreet.
A cat in glasses, reading a book,
While turtles skitter, our laughter they cook.

Every misstep a blissful surprise,
Like dancing with jellybeans, oh what a rise!
As echoes return in a whirlwind of laughs,
We find golden dreams in curious drafts.

Through these walls where giggles entwine,
Magic unfolds like a wondrous vine.
In this echoing chamber, we find our groove,
With each silly notion, our spirits we move.

Horizons of Hope

With cupcakes flying on candy clouds,
We giggle and wiggle, not lost in the crowds.
A surfboard of dreams rides the rainbow tide,
Where jellybean castles proudly reside.

As horizons stretch wide with splashes of cheer,
A parade of rubber ducks comes near.
We hop on the breeze with whimsical cheer,
In this land of laughter, there's nothing to fear.

We'misshape our worries like soft Puppy Pies,
While rainbows do cartwheels across clear skies.
Catch dreams in nets made of giggles and light,
For hope's just a giggle, oh what a sight!

With horizons so bright, we chase our own fate,
Through this fun-filled realm, let's dance and create.
So raise your glass high to the highs and the lows,
In this world of laughter, our spirit just glows!

The Heartbeat of Vision

In the attic of wishes, we soar quite high,
With a trampoline bed, we bounce to the sky.
The walls made of laughter, the ceiling of tunes,
Where socks turn to rocket ships, zooming by moons.

The kitchen's a circus, with pies that do flip,
The fridge sings a jingle, let's gather and sip.
Our pantry's a treasure, with candy galore,
Every snack tells a story, who could ask for more?

In the living room, gnomes have tea with a cat,
They debate about fashion—who's taller, who's fat?
The windows are portals to whacky new lands,
Where everything's silly and nothing still stands.

With dreams as our builders, we play and we cheer,
Our place full of giggles, there's nothing to fear.
So let's toast to the visions, both wild and absurd,
In our funny abode, let the laughter be heard.

Lanterns of Longing

A garden of wishes, we planted some joy,
With a swing made of rainbows, for each girl and boy.
The flowers do giggle, when tickled by breeze,
And butterflies dance like they're learning to tease.

At dusk we ignite, each lantern of dreams,
That flicker like stories, or wild, silly schemes.
They swirl and they hum, a delightfully mess,
Guiding our fantasies, we never know less.

In corners forgotten, a unicorn lives,
She plays hopscotch in shadows, and generously gives.
A parrot named Chuckles, he sings with flair,
While squirrels plot dramas, with popcorn to share.

When nighttime comes creeping, with snacks we unite,
Telling tales of our dreams, till the morning is bright.
With lanterns aglow, and silliness loud,
We leap into slumber, awesomely proud.

Breath of Inspiration

In a room full of doodles, ideas take flight,
While socks in the corners plot mischief at night.
The curtains are whispers, with secrets to tell,
About marshmallow clouds that we know oh so well.

A desk piled with treasures, both shiny and weird,
Where paperclip astronauts are boldly endeared.
The pens do a tango, while crayons take care,
To sketch dreams of cupcakes that float in midair.

We giggle with glee, over sketches and plans,
As marshmallows giggle and dance with their fans.
In a realm made of yarn, we craft every beat,
Each thread is a laughter that stirs in our seat.

When the clock strikes a joke, and midnight adds spice,
We'll laugh till we keel over—oh, isn't that nice?
With a breath of pure sunlight inspiring our schemes,
We dance to the rhythm of whimsy-filled dreams.

Tapestry of Tomorrow

Stitched with bright colors, tomorrow's our thread,
Where days dance like rainbows and chuckles are spread.
A quilt made of visions, we cozy up tight,
As fireflies giggle and twinkle in flight.

The chairs have opinions, they voice their delight,
While pillows hold meetings on how to nap right.
In corners we find, small gnomes with a plot,
To paint every shadow, and sprinkle some thought.

A hammock of wishes sways softly above,
Where dreams intertwine with the stories we love.
With stars for our guides, we'll travel afar,
By the light of our laughter, we'll reach every star.

So raise up your glasses, let's banter and giggle,
For a tapestry woven with joy in each wiggle.
With needle in hand, we can stitch and we'll sew,
Our tomorrows are wild—come along for the show!

Fields of Fantasia

In a field where wishes bloom,
A cow juggles, causing some gloom.
The sun wears shades, oh what a sight,
While butterflies dance in sheer delight.

A cat in a hat strums on a lute,
A pig learns the cha-cha, how cute!
Clouds play hide and seek with the sun,
In this land of laughter, oh what fun!

The trees tell tales of giggles and cheer,
While grasshoppers rap with no fear.
The flowers gossip, petals aflutter,
With bees that hum a sweet, silly stutter.

So come to the fields, leave worries behind,
Where joy is the currency, laughter's the find.
In this realm of whimsy, let's all play along,
For a world filled with fun is where we belong!

The Comfort of Creation

In a kitchen where chaos takes flight,
A dog wears an apron and cooks with delight.
Pancakes flop like a fish out of stream,
While toast sings a lullaby, a buttery dream.

The chef prances, a sprinkle of flour,
While cats take the stage in this cooking hour.
One sneaks the cake, another pulls a prank,
The blender roars, "I'm the star; don't you think?"

At the table, spoon fights erupt,
With jellybeans flying, and juice cups erupt.
Everyone giggles, avoids the sticky mess,
In this joyful kitchen, there's no room for stress.

So let's whip up fun with a dash of surprise,
With laughter as our secret ingredient prize.
In the comfort of creation, we all can play,
Turning ordinary moments into a delightful ballet!

Corners of Curiosity

In a nook where secrets like to hide,
A turtle dons glasses, filled with pride.
He reads books upside down, what a sight,
While owls hold court under the moonlight.

A broomstick races a squirrel on a spree,
While shadows dance quietly, sipping tea.
The carpet whispers tales of long lost friends,
In corners where whimsy never quite ends.

The plants do yoga, stretching so wide,
With cacti as critics, oh so snide.
Books giggle softly, pages flip-flop,
In the realm of the odd, there's always a hop.

So wander through corners with laughter in tow,
Where curiosity thrives, and imaginations glow.
In this playful world, let your mind take flight,
For in the corners of wonder, all things feel right!

The Loom of Longings

In the workshop of wishes where dreams take thread,
A spider makes sweaters for each tiny bed.
The yarn spins tales, higgledy-piggledy,
As gnomes sew socks while sipping on fig tea.

A raccoon's the tailor, crafty and spry,
With mismatched buttons that catch the eye.
Each stitch and each knot holds a story untold,
In this whimsical world, where dreams are bold.

A tapestry of laughter hangs on the wall,
With memories woven in a grand sprawl.
The looms click and clack, keeping time fine,
While creatures join in, each sip of divine.

So join in the weaving, let your heart sing,
In the loom of longings, life's a quirky thing.
With laughter and light, let's all play our part,
For in this vibrant yarn, we weave from the heart!

Frames of Freedom

In frames of laughter, we hang our thoughts,
With socks on the ceiling, and pants in knots.
A chorus of echoes, where giggles collide,
In the gallery of weird, we take so much pride.

Chasing after dreams that we sometimes forget,
With crayons and glitter, we dream with no fret.
The ticking of clocks says let's pause and play,
In this silly museum, let's dance our own way.

Couch cushions fortify, pillows serve as shields,
In battles of jest, our imagination yields.
With each playful clash, the world feels more bright,
In frames of our freedom, we soar into light.

The art of the crazy, the joy in the odd,
Like spaghetti on walls, it's bizarre but so broad.
In this framing of freedom, we chuckle and cheer,
For the quirks that unite us, our laughter is clear.

Gardens of Growth

In gardens where mischief and laughter sprout,
We plant all our secrets, but watch out for doubt.
A swing hanging low, a slide made of dreams,
Where flowers of giggles burst forth at the seams.

Watering with puns, we watch humor unfold,
With daisies of wisdom, and sunflowers bold.
Each blossom a tale, each leaf a new plan,
In our verdant escape, yes, we smile like fans.

The weeds of worry, we pull with a laugh,
Creating our joy, we're the garden's own staff.
A maze made of humor, a path full of glee,
In growth that is funny, we bloom wild and free.

As veggies play hide and seek in the sun,
With carrots in costumes, the party's begun.
In this patch of delight, where nonsense is sown,
We harvest the laughter, we've all overgrown.

Doorways to Delight

Behind each door lies a riddle or joke,
Where silliness lingers and laughter's bespoke.
With door knobs that giggle and hinges that sing,
Every opening's charm is a wondrous fling.

A door to the kitchen? Oh, what could it hide?
With cookies and cupcakes, come on, let's collide!
Through passageways painted in colors so bright,
We learn that the awkward is often our right.

Each threshold a story, a twist in the tale,
Of adventures that wobble, and ships that set sail.
In the halls of our home, let the echoes resound,
With every sweet knock, more delight to be found.

Old doors squeak wisdom, while new ones have flair,
In doorways to delight, it's a merry affair.
Let's trip on adventures, let's laugh till we fall,
For surely, we'll find joy in each turn of the hall.

Spaces of Solitude

In corners of quiet, where silliness grows,
We nestle our thoughts in a blanket of prose.
Surrounded by cushions of comfort and cheer,
In spaces of solitude, let's chuckle sincere.

With teacups that giggle and books that surprise,
Each moment a secret, each glance like sunrise.
A fortress of laughter, where worries take flight,
In stillness, we find we can dance in the night.

The echoes of solitude wrap us like wool,
Where deviled eggs joke and the cats make us drool.
In silence so sweet, where rhymes can take hold,
We laugh with our thoughts, let the doubts all be sold.

A space for the quirky, where dreams often thrive,
With stripes on the walls, we feel so alive.
In this quirky retreat, let's laugh and let go,
For solitude's humor, we cherish and grow.

The Cornice of Creativity

On a roof made of ideas, they dance and play,
With colors so bright, they'd scare clouds away.
A cat with a hat sits sipping on tea,
While the goldfish recites poetry under a tree.

Invisible llamas wear spectacles too,
Sipping their smoothies, in shades of bright blue.
The curtains are giggling, the floorboards all sing,
In this jolly old space where joy's the main thing.

Balloons float around like wise old men,
Whispering secrets, then popping again.
The kitchen is lively, the fridge tells a joke,
While the toaster gets feisty—watch out for the smoke!

Here every odd clock has a tale to unfold,
With tick-tocky rhythm that isn't too bold.
As laughter erupts from beneath fluffy beds,
This whimsical place fills your heart up instead.

Labyrinths of Light

In a maze of bright colors, oh what a sight,
A squirrel on a skateboard zooms left and right.
He chats with a lamp post, they swap silly puns,
While shadows do the cha-cha, oh what fun runs!

Glittery corridors spiral like candy,
Each twist fills your heart and feelings get dandy.
The mirrors are giggling, reflecting our grins,
As a polka-dotted chihuahua learns how to spin.

Upside-down umbrellas drift lazily high,
They float in the air, just like wishes in the sky.
With sunshine that tickles and laughter that shines,
Together we dance, tangled in whimsical vines.

So here in this maze, there's no need for maps,
Just follow the giggles and enjoy all the naps.
Each corner you turn, brings a new wacky sight,
In labyrinths of light, every moment's a delight!

The Hearth of Hopes

At the hearth where dreams brew a curious stew,
The chairs sing out like a whimsical crew.
With socks made of laughter and slippers of glee,
They toast to the table where sandwiches flee.

A puppy is chef, wearing a tall, goofy hat,
He juggles the apples, while dancing with a cat.
The oven's a dragon, breathing out warm sighs,
As marshmallows giggle and play with the pies.

In this kitchen of wonders, the fridge hums a tune,
While the windows grow windowsill flowers in June.
Stories bubble up like a frothy fond dream,
As the spoons tell each other, "Let's form a team!"

So gather around, let your worries all float,
In the hearth of our hopes, we'll add a pinch of smote.
With spices of laughter and sprinkles of cheer,
We'll feast on our dreams, and toast with good beer!

Streams of Imagination

In a river of thoughts, where silliness flows,
A crocodile surfboards in bright rainbows.
With jellybean tides and marzipan rocks,
The fish wear bow ties and converse with the clocks.

As paper boats sail, made of wishes and fears,
They tell of adventures and glittering years.
Each ripple a giggle, each splash a bright cheer,
In the streams of imagination, all things are clear.

Now come ride the waves of whimsical fun,
With fruitcake submarines and gumdrops to run.
The sun's made of candy, the moon's a big cake,
And every odd moment, a new dream we'll make.

So let's float together, no map, just delight,
In the streams of our dreams, we'll soar with our flight.
With mermaids made of paper and unicorns brave,
We'll dance through the currents, forever we'll wave!